Railtour in colour

First published 1976.

ISBN 07110 0676 8

Cover, front: Jubilee No 5596 *Bahamas* of the Bahamas Locomotive Society heading a Manchester-Sheffield special near Chinley in June 1973. *(R. E. B. Siviter)*; **back above:** Leighton Buzzard Light Railway's de Winton 0-4-0 *Chaloner* near Stanbridge Road on March 30 1970; **back below:** ex-National Coal Board 0-6-2T No 29 on the North Yorkshire Moors line in June 1970. *J. M. Boyes*

Below: An evening sky silhouetting a Terrier tank and its train as it crossed Langstone Harbour Bridge on the former LBSCR Havant-Hayling Island branch in 1963.

PUBLISHED BY

IAN ALLAN LTD

TERMINAL HOUSE·SHEPPERTON·TW17 8AS·ENGLAND
TELEPHONE: WALTON-ON-THAMES 28484

Printed by Crampton & Sons Ltd, Sawston, Cambridge

Stanier Class 8 2-8-0 No 48442 heading a
Gowhole-Buxton freight at Chinley South Junction
on February 3 1968. *D. Huntriss*

THIS book is published to serve the evergreen demand for good railway pictures and particularly for colour pictures of steam railways as they used to be. All the pictures have been published before in Ian Allan magazines or books, but it has enabled us to produce a unique collection of four-colour pictures on high-quality paper at a very modest price. The scenes herein portrayed fall generally into three main categories, but they are not assembled strictly into groups. The categories covered are trains normally at work on British Rail during the last few years before the end of steam; railtour and open day activities of the preservation societies and their restored locomotives; and operations on some of the preserved railways. One or two good industrial shots add variety.

Mostly, the pictures are of home scenes, but two of the most famous of British steam locomotives, *Flying Scotsman* and *Repton*, are shown in the United States; *Repton* of course is now owned by an American society but No 4472 was happily rescued and returned to its homeland from a doubtful future there after the financial failure of its American tour a few years ago. One foreigner allowed in is Steamtown's French 231K Pacific for its Golden Arrow connections.

Similarly, most of the scenes show steam locomotives but, to please the growing number of railway devotees who ask for more of the 'modern stuff', there is a leavening of electric- and diesel-worked trains from the collection of good colour pictures by photographers among our regular contributors.

Altogether, the book presents a nostalgic and colourful kaleidoscope of Britain's railways and railway vehicles in their infinite variety. Preserved railways such as the Bluebell, Dart Valley, Keighley & Worth Valley, Severn Valley and the Welsh narrow-gauge lines are featured, as are the important enthusiast centres of Didcot, Tyseley and Carnforth.

Such perennial favourites as *Joem, Green Arrow, Earl of Berkeley* and *Sir Nigel Gresley* are to be seen, not to mention a fascinating collection of Castle, Hall, Class 5, Jubilee, Terrier and many other well-known and lesser-known gems.

Former SECR Class H 0-4-4T No 31308 leaving Three Bridges with a Sunday push-pull train to East Grinstead in October 1962. *G. D. King*

BR Standard Class 4 4-6-0 No 75077 makes a fine spectacle assaulting the 1 in 60 of Parkstone Bank shortly after leaving Poole with the through York train in March 1967, a few months before the demise of steam operation on the Southern. *R. D. White*

Romney Hythe & Dymchurch No 10 *Dr Syn* in full cry
on a supporters' association special at Burmarsh Road
on September 20 1970.   *T. Miller*

Below: The Brighton Belle in its original umber and cream Pullman livery crossing the Ouse Viaduct en route for Brighton in the summer of 1963.
P. W. Simmonds

Right: On October 3 1972, Class 74 electro-diesel locomotive No E6101 (now 71.001) approaching Southampton Eastern Docks with an Ocean Liner Express from Waterloo conveying passengers for ss *France.* *R. Parr*

Left: Bulleid Pacific No 35028 *Clan Line* of the Merchant Navy Locomotive Preservation Society, nearing Warminster with the steam special between Basingstoke and Westbury on April 27 1974. The train was hauled by an electro-diesel between Waterloo and Basingstoke. *J. H. Cooper-Smith*

Below: LSWR Drummond T9 Class 4-4-0 No 120 approaching Christ's Hospital from the Guildford branch with the LCGB Sussex Coast Limited railtour on June 24 1962. *G. D. King*

Right: Ex-Southern Railway S15 class 4-6-0 No 841 (BR No 30841) in steam at Chappel & Wakes Colne, headquarters of the Stour Valley Railway Preservation Society, on July 21 1974, just after its restoration to Southern livery. It is here illustrated during a second steaming. *G. D. King.*

Below right: Former Southern Railway Schools class 4-4-0 No 926 *Repton* in 1974 crossing a trestle bridge on the Cape Breton Steam Railway, Nova Scotia, to which it was then on loan from its present owner Steamtown Museum, USA. *Robin Russell*

Northern Ireland Railway 2-6-4T No 4 and privately
preserved GNRI Class S 4-4-0 *Slieve Gullion*
double-heading a Railway Preservation Society of
Ireland's Brian Boru railtour starting out of Cork over
Six Arch viaduct, near Rathpeacon, in 1969.
G. M. Kichenside

No 4 *Loch* of the Isle of Man Railway arriving at
Port St Mary beneath a welcoming banner on August
13 1973, during the IOM Railway centenary
celebrations.   *Klaus Marx*

Stanier Class 5 4-6-0 No 45352 leaving the Tubular
Bridge and running past the ramparts of Conway
Castle with a Manchester-Bangor express on August
28 1964.   *Derek Cross*

WR Castle Class 4-6-0 No 5090 *Neath Abbey*
heading the 15.15 Paddington to Worcester past
Reading on October 28 1961.   *J. W. Millbank*

Left: Standard Class 4 2-6-4T
No 80032 leaving Redhill for
Tonbridge in April 1964.
G. D. King

Below: GW 61xx Class 2-6-2T
No 6129 nearing Banbury with a
local train on the WR Paddington-
Birmingham line in April 1964.
J. A. Kirke

Right: Stanier Class 5 4-6-0
No 45926 climbing towards Shap
Summit with a Morecambe-
Glasgow excursion on September
28 1964. *Derek Cross*

Below right: Preserved GWR
Castle class 4-6-0 No 4079
Pendennis Castle passing
Marshbrook Crossing, between
Hereford and Shrewsbury, with a
steam special in 1975.
M. J. P. Tyack

Below: A Class 25 locomotive passing through Newport with a block coal train bound for the London Midland Region. *British Rail*

Right: A Class 52 skirting the sea wall at Teignmouth at the head of an express for the West of England. *W. R. Whittle*

Left: LNER D3 class 4-4-0 No 2000 (ex-GNR) running in 1948. This particular engine was normally used for railway officers' specials, and was the only member of the class restored to LNER green after 1945. *J. M. Jarvis*

Above: A BR standard Class 5 4-6-0 climbing towards the Shap Summit during the last week of steam working on the West Coast main line in 1967. *B. A. Reeves*

Above left: Restored V2 class 2-6-2 No 4771 *Green Arrow* on Hatton Bank approaching Warwick on June 24 1973.   *G. J. Hilton*

Left: A4 Pacific No 4498 *Sir Nigel Gresley* heading an LCGB Gresley Commemorative Special from Tyseley to Didcot out of Harbury Tunnel in July 1973.
J. H. Cooper-Smith

Above: No 4472 *Flying Scotsman* climbing the last lap to Shap Summit on June 29 1969, hauling a North Eastern Locomotive Preservation Group railtour from Newcastle to the Keighley & Worth Valley Railway via York and Leeds.   *J. W. Jackson*

Above left: An early morning scene at Perth in 1962, with LMR Coronation Pacific No 48244 *King George VI* accelerating a train of vans after a check.

T. Russell

Left: The late afternoon sun catches Class 4 4-6-0 No 75030 as it banks a freight on the climb to Shap on December 9 1967.   *A. Stewart*

Above: Stanier Class 8 2-8-0 No 48448 storming towards Copy Pit with an early morning freight to Burnley on February 24 1968.   *A. Stewart*

Class 5 4-6-0 No 44713 approaching Burscough Junction with the 16.53 Preston-Liverpool Exchange on April 7 1968.   *J. E. Berry*

Jubilee 4-6-0 No 45711 *Courageous* heading a
Saturday Heads of Ayr-Leeds train at Ais Gill summit
on August 29 1959.   *J. G. Tawse*

Ex-LMS Jubilee 4-6-0 No 5596 *Bahamas*, of the
Bahamas Locomotive Society, Dinting, heading a
Manchester to Sheffield special near Chinley Junction
on June 17 1973.   *R. E. B. Siviter*

D16 4-4-0 No 62570 pulling away from Swavesey, on the Cambridge-March St Ives Loop line, with a Cambridge to Birmingham train in the autumn of 1959. *G. D. King*

Privately preserved LNER Class A3 Pacific No 4472
Flying Scotsman passing Drem Junction with a
Scunthorpe-Edinburgh excursion on June 25 1967.
Derek Cross

Above: *Flying Scotsman* in Jefferson Street, San Francisco, near Fisherman's Wharf, on its way to begin revenue passenger service on the San Francisco Belt Railroad on March 18 1972—the first steam working and the first passenger train on the line since World War 2.   *Thomas A. Acheson*

Below: *Flying Scotsman* at work on the SFBR. The San Francisco-Oakland Bay Bridge can be seen in the background of the picture.

Thomas A. Acheson

Austerity 2-8-0 No 90508 in full cry in an autumn
landscape, the plume of its exhaust compensating for
its lacklustre black paint. *A. Stewart*

Class Q6 0-8-0 No 63397 tackling the 1 in 50 of
Hesledon bank near Monk Hesledon village with a
West Hartlepool-Thornley Colliery mineral empties
train on the cold winter's morning of February 8 1967.
J. M. Boyes

Above: A three-car cross-country dmu nearing Luffenham on a Birmingham-Leicester-Peterborough working on September 16 1970. *D. Bradley*

Right: A Leeds-Manchester dmu service approaching Standedge Tunnel at Marsden. *J. H. Cooper-Smith*

Above: *Lydham Manor* heading the Torbay Steam Railway's 15.00 Paignton-Kingswear near Goodrington on April 7 1974 carries a headboard specially made from an original in the Clapham Museum.

Peter Zabek

Above right: The Dart Valley Railway's GW 2-6-2T No 4555 climbing out of Paignton with a special to Kingswear on July 30 1972 during timetable trials and public trips preparatory to operation of the line by the DVR as the Torbay Steam Railway.

G. Daniels

Right: The Dart Valley Railway's ex-GW 2-6-2T No 4588, shortly after its overhaul at Swindon, approaching Staverton Bridge on September 12 1971 with a BR through excursion from Swansea to Buckfastleigh. *J. W. Millbank*

Army Department 2-10-0 No 600 *Gordon* in spotless
condition leaving Liss Forest Road on the Longmoor
Military Railway on July 5 1969. *Gordon* is retained
in working order on the Severn Valley Railway at
Bridgnorth. *R. D. White*

The Kent & East Sussex Railway's Terrier 0-6-0T
No 10 *Sutton* showing its paces on the 1 in 50
Tenterden Bank.   *A. L. Newble*

Left: Former SECR Class P 0-6-0T No 27 shunting a two-coach train of SECR stock at Horsted Keynes on the Bluebell Railway. *J. H. Bird*

Below left: The fireman of GW 4-4-0 No 3217 on the Bluebell handing over the staff to the Horsted Keynes signalman after arrival from Sheffield Park.

J. H. Bird

Right: Former LBSCR No 55 *Stepney* and North London 0-6-0T No 2650 standing at Horsted Keynes after arrival from Sheffield Park. *G. D. King*

Below: The Bluebell Railway's ex-L&SWR Adams 4-4-2T, once BR No 30583, at Sheffield Park: also visible are the ex-GWR Dukedog 4-4-0 No 9017 and an ex-SECR P class 0-6-0T.

J. B. Snell

Above: J27 0-6-0T No 69023 *Joem* heading into the setting sun as it climbs towards Ingrow with the last train from Keighley to Oxenhope on the Keighley & Worth Valley Railway on November 29 1969.

A Stewart

Above right: Ivatt 2-6-2T No 41241 and USA 0-6-0T No 72 approaching Oxenhope with a Santa Special on December 20 1970. *A. Stewart*

Right: One of the Keighley & Worth Valley's four 0-6-0STs pulling into Oakworth. *J. D. Mills*

Above left: Interlude in a busy life in retirement, No 7029 *Clun Castle* at Tyseley on May 2 1971.

A. L. Newble

Left: GWR King class No 6000 *King George V* reviving memories of Paddington-Birmingham two-hour expresses as it climbs Hatton Bank, making for Tyseley on October 2 1971, first day of a week-long tour with the Bulmers Cider Pullman train.

D. Huntriss

Above: LNER No 4771 *Green Arrow* standing at Morecambe in August 1973, with moonlight rippling along the rich green of its boiler and firebox.

A. Oldfield

Above left: A general view of Didcot depot of the GW Preservation Society on the members' open day on May 2 1970. *G. R. Hounsell*

Left: The Great Western Society's preserved 0-4-2T No 1466 propelling an auto-train to Wallingford on one of the society open days in 1968.
Brian Stephenson

Above: A picturesque scene on the Dart Valley Railway; one of the company's 0-4-2T locomotives with an auto trailer crosses the Dart Bridge near Buckfastleigh. *John Adams*

Left: Leighton Buzzard Light Railway's de Winton 0-4-0 *Chaloner* near Stanbridge Road on March 30 1970.

Below: Stanier Class 5 4-6-0 No 45110 heading the 12.00 from Bridgnorth on September 20 1970, the first time the engine had been used on passenger services on the Severn Valley, and since it worked the last BR special in 1968.
T. Bending

Above left: Ivatt Class 2 2-6-0 No 46521 leaving Knowlesands Tunnel on the Severn Valley Railway. *M. R. Wilkins*

Left: Isle of Man Railway 2-4-0T No 12 *Hutchinson* passing Devil's Elbow with a Douglas-Ramsey train on June 21 1968. *G. D. King*

Left: Former NBC 0-6-2T No 29 heading a train between Grosmont and Goathland on the North Yorkshire Moors line on June 28 1970. *J. M. Boyes*

Below left: Ex-Lambton Colliery 0-6-0T No 29, built by Kitson in 1904, climbing towards Goathland with a train from Grosmont on the North Yorkshire Moors Railway. *Ivo Peters*

Below: British Aluminium Co's Peckett 0-4-0T at Burntisland, Fife, in 1967. *Derek Cross*

Bottom: Scottish Malt Distillers Barclay 0-4-0T at Cromdale in 1967. *J. M. Boyes*

Left: Carnforth Steamtown's B1 4-6-0 No 1306 in LNER green with pre-Thomson shaded lettering.
J. D. Mills

Below left: Steamtown's SNCF Pacific 231K22, rebuilt in 1937 from a PLM locomotive, one of the class that worked the Golden Arrow between Calais and the electrified section at Amiens after the war.
Derek Cross

Below: LNW Precedent 2-4-0 *Hardwicke*, veteran of the Race to the North in 1895, when visiting Steamtown from Clapham Museum in 1974 for its Locomotion 74 gathering.
Derek Cross

The Peterborough Railway Society's BR Standard
Class 5 4-6-0 No 73050 *City of Peterborough* making
an appearance at one of the society's steam weekends
in March 1973.   *Ray D. Clarke*

On March 29 1970 privately preserved SECR Class 01
0-6-0 No 65 was steamed at Ashford; it is seen here
shunting up and down the yard at Ashford with one
of the Pullman cars aslo stabled there. *M. Morant*

Above left: BR Class 40 No 345 with a breakdown crane leaving Blea Moor tunnel on February 17 1973.
J. H. Cooper-Smith

Left: General view of Kings Cross Station with Deltic Class 55 No 9004 winding its way through the tortuous layout with the *Flying Scotsman* for Edinburgh on May 1 1972. *J. H. Cooper-Smith*

Above: Class 86 No 86.022 heading a Freightliner train near Lichfield on the West Coast main line.
David M. Cross

The rebuilt LMS *Royal Scot* locomotive No 6100, first
of its class, at Bressingham Steam Museum.
M. L. Williams

Of the three LNER A4 Pacifics in private ownership in this country only one, No 60009 *Union of South Africa,* is able to run freely since it is used on the Lochty Private Railway in Fife, Scotland. No 60009 is seen here in June 1970 with the former Coronation observation car leaving Lochty Station.

Derek Cross

Above: Caledonian livery lives again, unexpectedly,
on Lakeside & Haverthwaite's ex-BR 2-6-4T No 2085.
J. D. Mills

Below: Festiniog Railway Fairlie 0-4-4-0T *Earl of
Merioneth* leaving Portmadoc during the summer of
1970. *D. R. Whitnell*

Robert Stephenson & Hawthorns 0-6-0ST No 39
heading away from Foxfield banked by Bagnall
0-4-0ST *J. T. Daly* during an operating day on the
Foxfield Light Railway.   *A. Stewart*

Vale of Rheidol 2-6-2T No 7 *Owain Glyndwr* climbing towards Devils Bridge on April 7 1969.   *D. Huntriss*

Welshpool & Llanfair Light Railway's Beyer-Peacock
0-6-0T *The Earl* of 1903 leaving Sylfaen with a train
to Llanfair Caereinion on April 20 1973.
R. E. B. Siviter

National Coal Board 0-4-0T No 21 of the West Ayr
area shunting NCB coal wagons at Waterside Colliery
on March 2 1965.   *Derek Cross*